The Cat Came Back

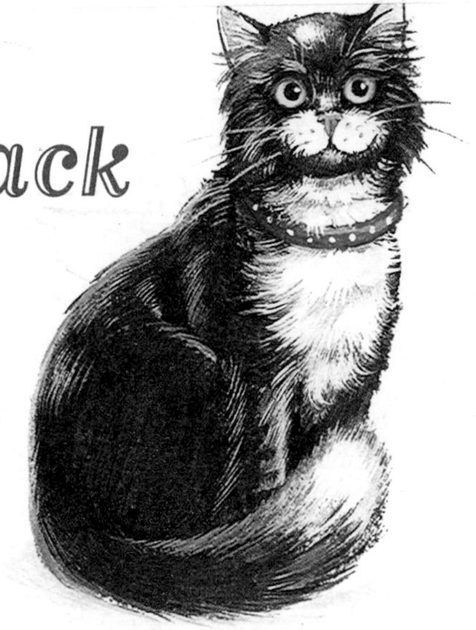

Written by Carly Easton
Illustrated by Krista Brauckmann-Towns

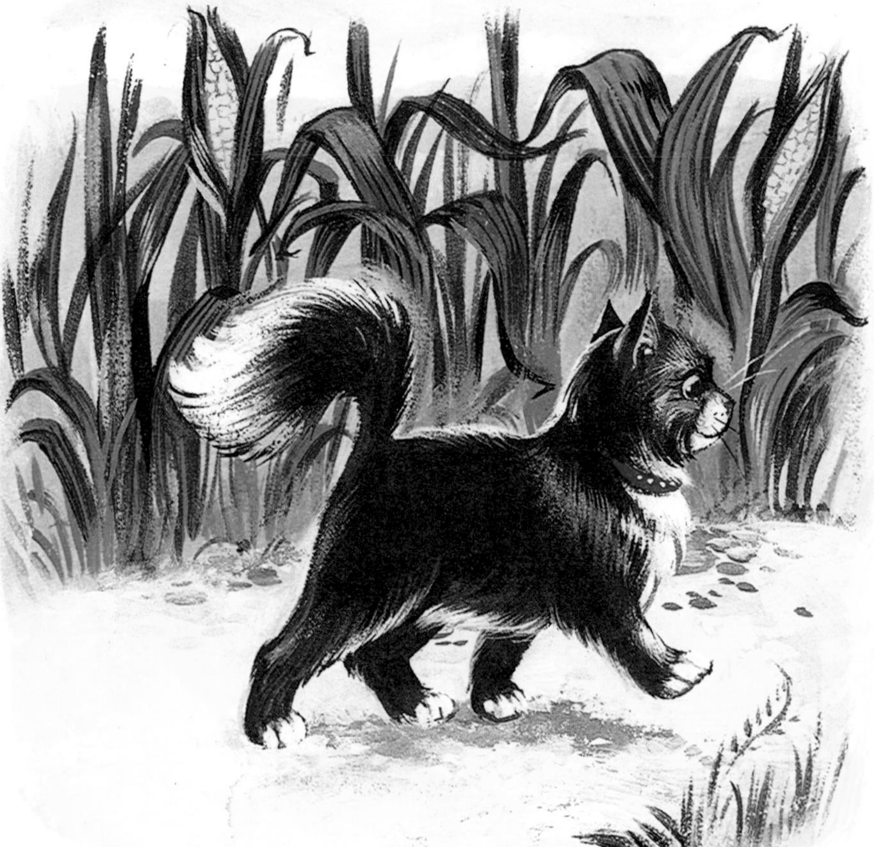

By the corn,

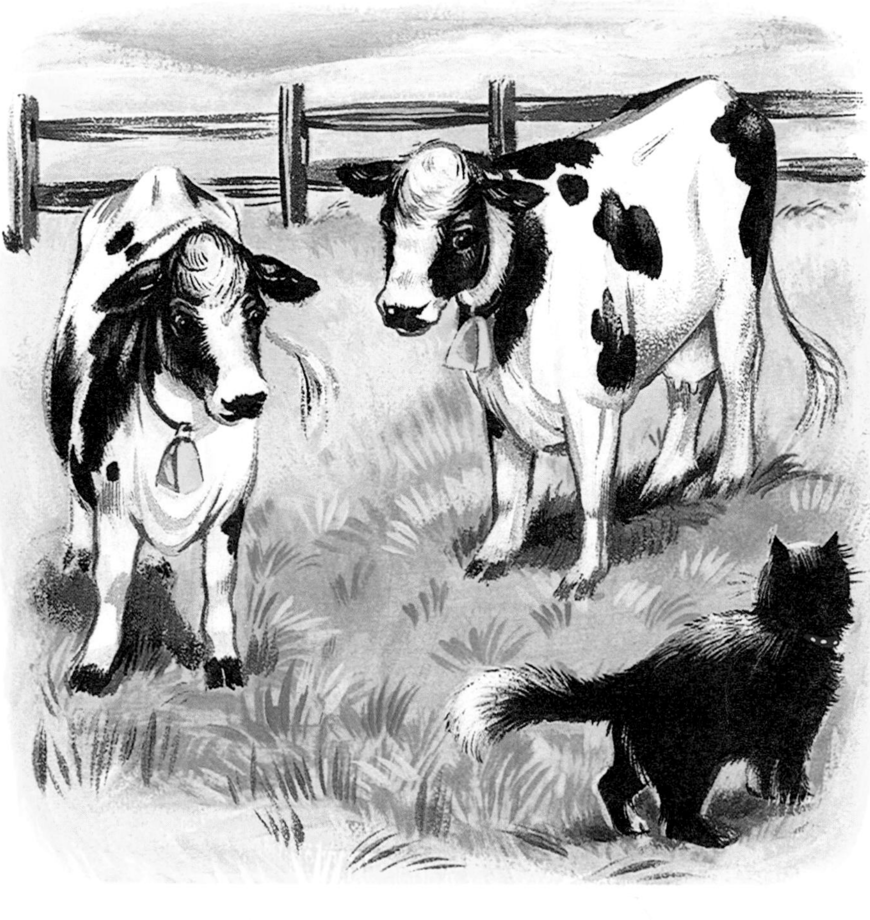

by the cows,

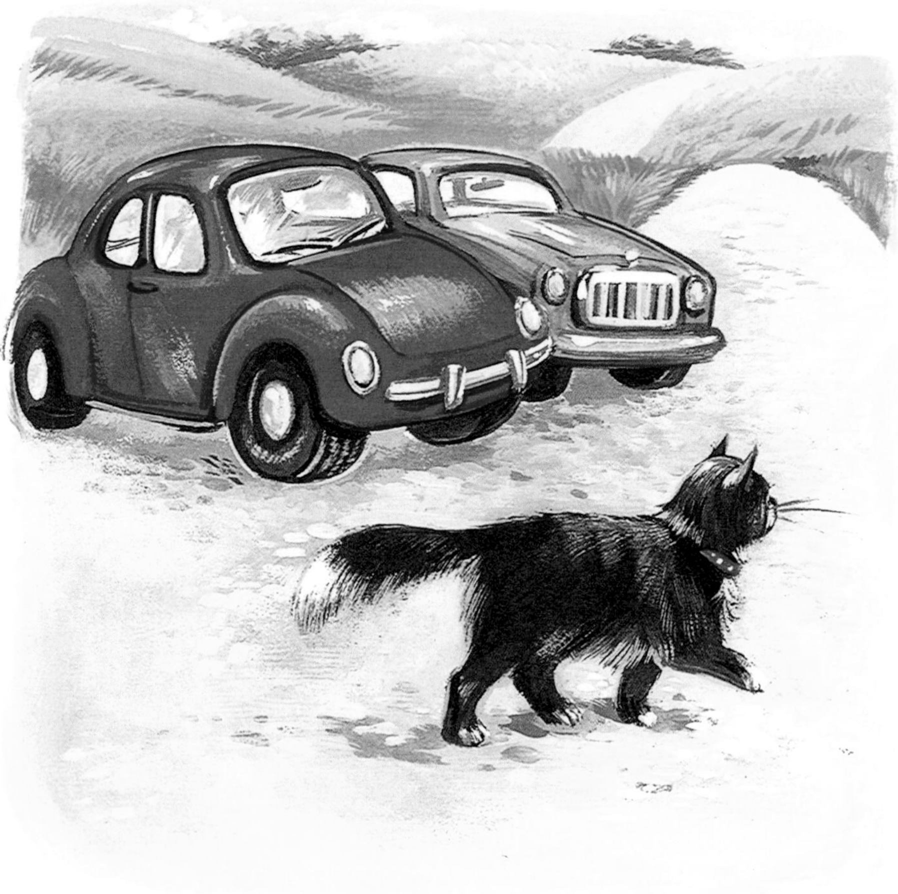

by the cars,

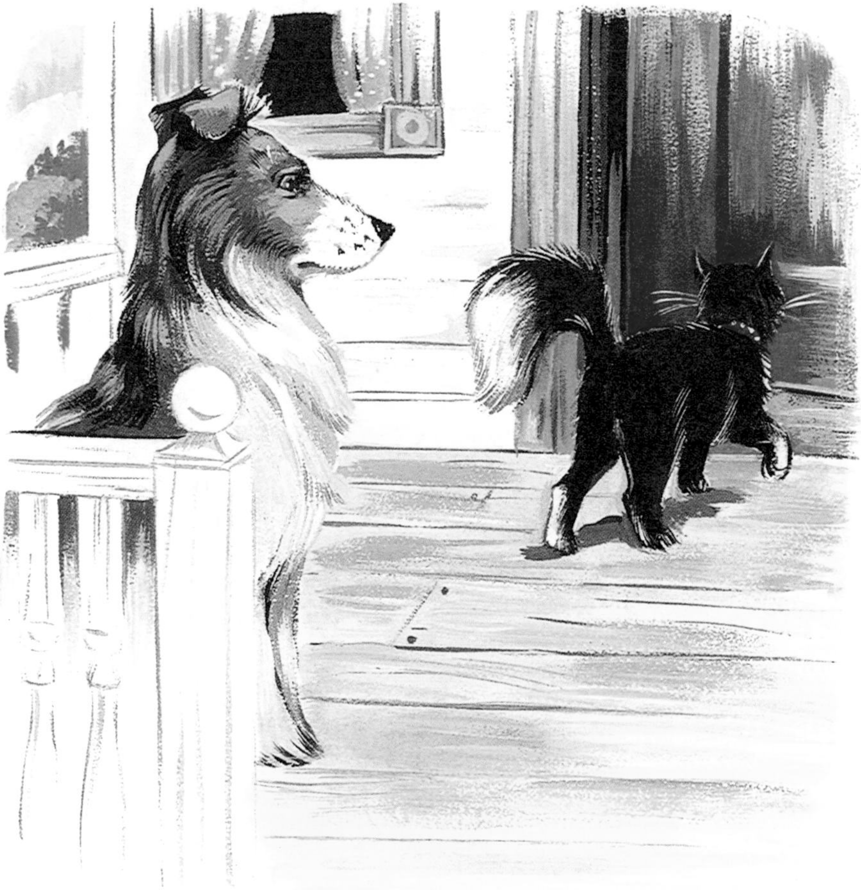

by the dog,

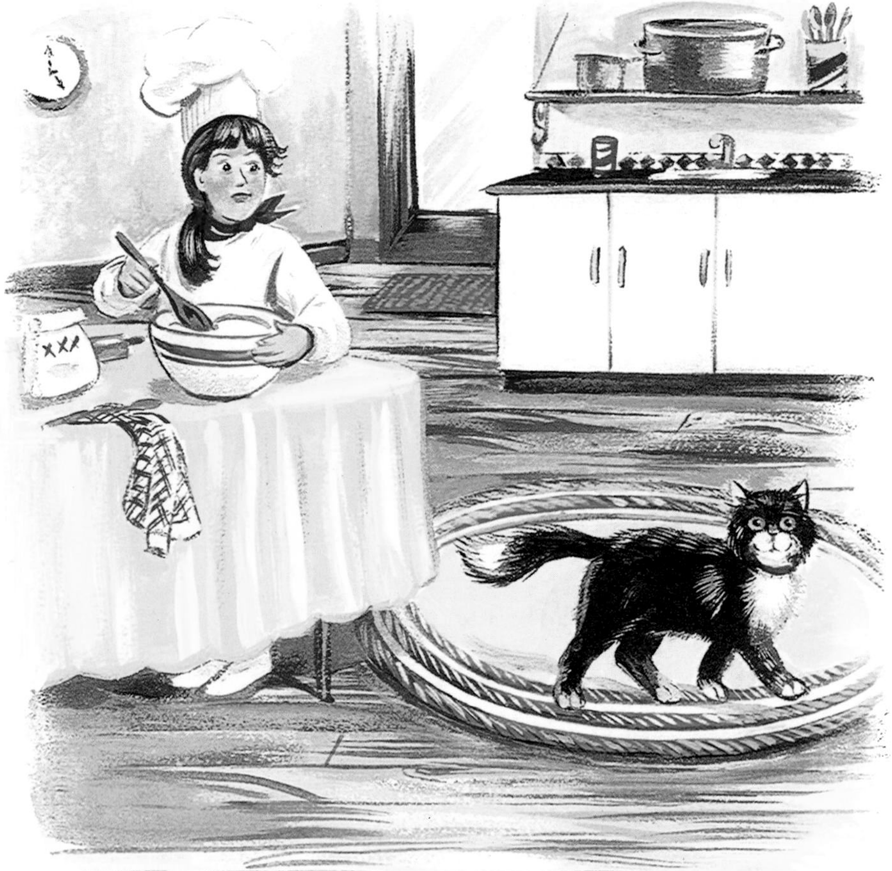

by the cook,

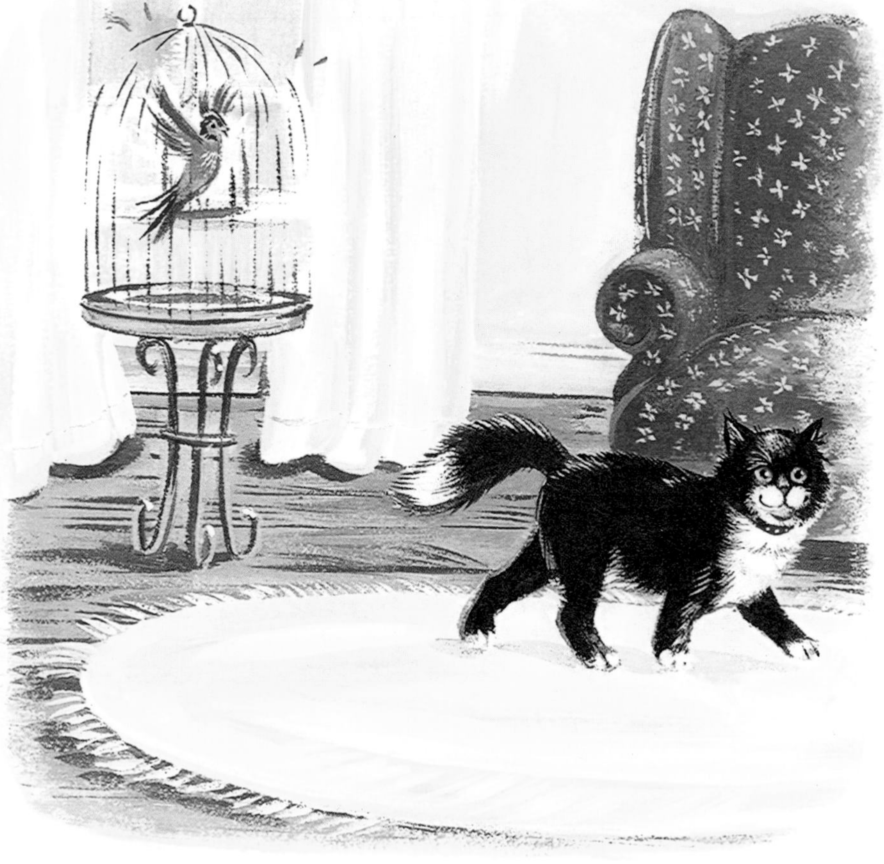

by the bird.

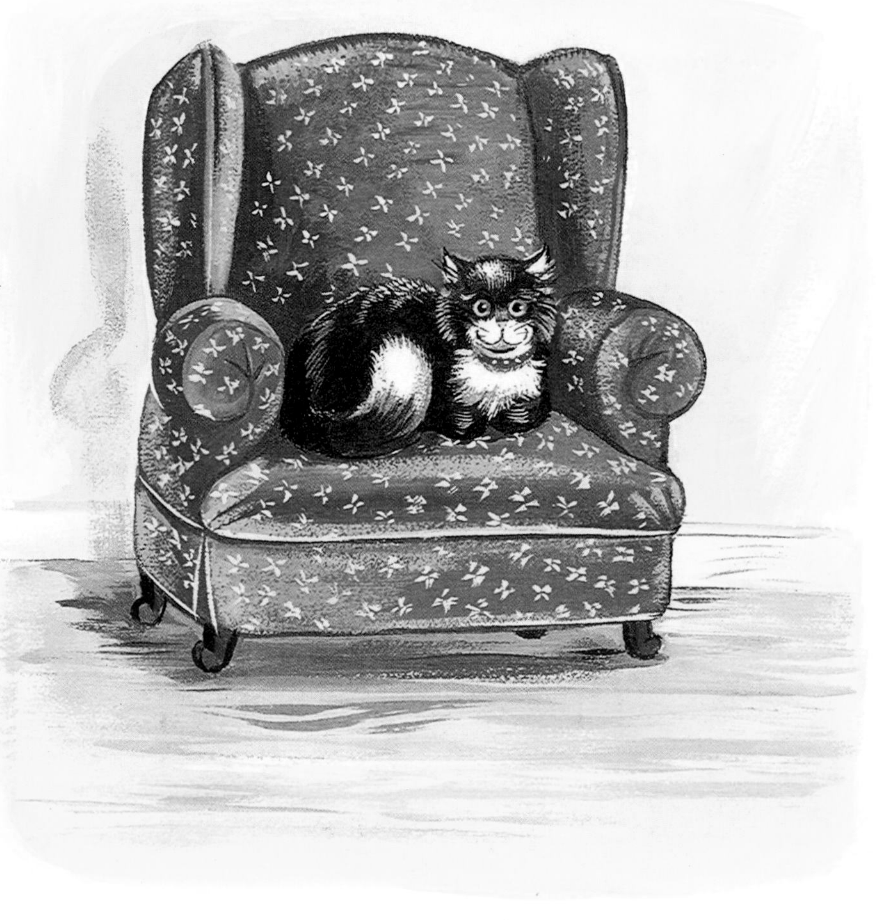

The cat came back.